- 02 **Introduction**
- 06 Chapter One: **Empathy**
  The Spirit of Service Excellence
- 11 Chapter Two: **Effective Communication**
  Bridging Connections
- 17 Chapter Three: **Adaptability**
  No Two Days are the same
- 23 Chapter Four: **Positive Attitude**
  The Power of Optimism
- 29 Chapter Five: **Patience**
  The Art of Composure
- 35 Chapter Six: **Problem-Solving**
  Navigating Challenges
- 43 Chapter Seven: **Attention to Detail**
  Perfecting the Experience
- 51 Chapter Eight: **Resilience**
  The Quiet Strength
- 58 Chapter Nine: **Teamwork**
  The Muscle Power
- 65 Chapter Ten: **Continuous Learning**
  Evolving Excellence

Introduction

Imagine a bustling city hotel, alive with energy on the eve of a major international conference. Amid the flurry of activity, a guest steps in — visibly tense, clutching documents, and navigating messages on their phone.

Immediately, the front desk agent senses the pressure and responds with a calm, genuine smile. With an expert's grace, she checks him in swiftly, arranges a quiet workspace nearby equipped with high-speed internet, and thoughtfully adds refreshments for comfort.

Throughout the evening, she checks in with discreet warmth, offering to print last-minute documents or bring a light snack.

Meanwhile, the concierge team is carefully preparing his meeting space, noting every detail to ensure it meets his needs. When he finally arrives at his room, he's greeted by a pristine, calming space — crisp linens, a soft bed, and a handwritten note from the team, wishing him success.

This is the essence of the human touch in hospitality — the intuitive ability to transform tension into comfort, stress into calm, and every interaction into a lasting impression of warmth and reliability.

Hospitality isn't merely a business; it's a world where the art of service thrives, powered by genuine connections that touch the heart and elevate the spirit.

At its core is service excellence, where every interaction transcends the routine and becomes an extraordinary exchange.

Think back to a moment when service felt like more than just a transaction, when you felt truly seen and understood. In a world where AI can process requests with speed and precision, we must ask: can technology replicate the warmth of a kind smile or the comfort of a thoughtful gesture?

This dedication to personal connection not only shapes the guest experience but defines the lasting success of hospitality.

While AI can enhance efficiency, it is human insight that makes a guest feel truly valued.

A skilled host senses needs before they're voiced, turns details into delights, and creates an atmosphere of authentic care.

In this book, we'll explore the irreplaceable qualities of service excellence and the power of the human touch.

We'll uncover how these qualities not only elevate guest experiences but drive the long-term success of hospitality establishments.

Join us on a journey to discover what it truly means to serve with empathy, intuition, and the heart of hospitality.

Chapter One: Empathy

The Spirit of Service Excellence

There are ten essential human qualities that define true service excellence, and at the forefront of these, is empathy — a trait that lies at the heart of every meaningful guest interaction. Like a guiding spirit, empathy infuses each moment with understanding, care, and a deep connection that transcends the ordinary.

Empathy, at its core, is the ability to step into someone else's shoes, to see and feel the world as they do.

In the hospitality industry, where every interaction has the potential to profoundly impact a guest's experience, empathy becomes the bridge that connects service to genuine care.

It is the spirit that animates every gesture, word, and decision, ensuring that guests feel truly seen, understood, and valued.

A weary elderly guest, fatigued from the previous day's activities, tussles into the dining area during a busy breakfast buffet.

An observant waiter, recognizing the guest's discomfort, offers attentive table service, remembering the guest's favorite items from the day before.

This thoughtful act not only eases the guest's burden but also exemplifies the core of service excellence — where empathy is woven into every interaction, making each moment a reflection of the care that defines true hospitality.

Now, imagine another guest who is celebrating a special occasion, such as an anniversary. The waiter, after overhearing the reason for the visit, takes the opportunity to acknowledge the milestone with a personal touch.

They might suggest a special dessert or arrange for a small celebratory gesture, such as a handwritten note from the restaurant's staff.

This level of personalized service, driven by empathy, turns the guest's meal into a memorable celebration, reflecting a genuine understanding of their joy.

Here, empathy is not just a fleeting moment of kindness; it is the enduring spirit that turns service into memories, where every interaction is tailored to the guest's emotional landscape.

It's about anticipating and addressing the deeper, often unspoken needs of each guest.

Whether it's handling a complaint with sensitivity, offering comfort during a difficult moment, or simply recognizing and celebrating a special occasion, empathy elevates service from routine to exceptional.

When hospitality professionals apply empathy with sincerity and care, they elevate service to an art form, creating moments that guests will remember long after they've left.

In the end, it is empathy that breathes life into service, transforming it from a transaction into a connection, from a duty into a heartfelt commitment to making every guest feel valued and cared for."

Building on empathy, effective communication is the conduit that links understanding with action.

Clear and considerate communication ensures that the insights gained through empathy are accurately conveyed and acted upon.

Chapter Two: **Effective Communication**

Bridging Connections

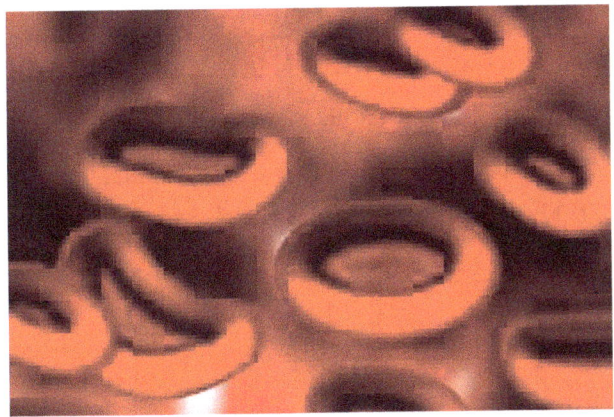

Effective communication is the lifeblood of service excellence in hospitality, essential for fueling every interaction and enhancing the guest experience.

Just as oxygen energizes the body, allowing it to perform at its peak, effective communication invigorates the guest experience, ensuring it not only meets expectations but exceeds them.

It's not only about the words spoken but also the tone, the gestures, and even the silences that shape the interaction.

Mastering both verbal and non-verbal cues is crucial to creating a welcoming, seamless experience that makes each guest feel genuinely valued and fully understood.

Picture a scene at a busy hotel check-in counter. A guest arrives, visibly exhausted after a long journey, and their mood hints at weariness or irritability. The front desk agent, perceptive and experienced, recognizes the guest's state and offers a warm smile with a calm, reassuring tone.

The agent's greeting, "Welcome! How was your journey?" may seem simple, but the way it's delivered — gentle, genuine, and accompanied by open posture and slight forward lean — signals attentiveness and a readiness to assist. In that moment, the guest's tension dissipates.

They feel truly seen, their concerns acknowledged. Here, effective verbal and non-verbal communication merge like oxygen flowing seamlessly through the body, enriching every element of the experience.

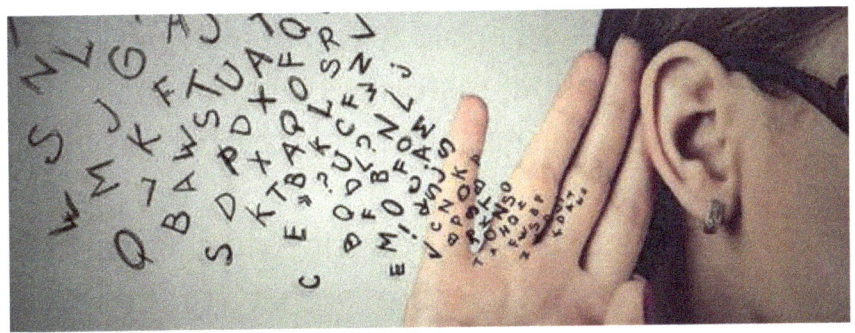

Contrast this with a different approach. The same guest arrives at the counter, but the agent, although using the right words, speaks in a rushed tone, making minimal eye contact.

Perhaps the agent is typing on the computer while talking, or their body language seems closed off, arms crossed or posture stiff. Though the words are correct, the tone and demeanor send a different message: the guest is not the priority.

The guest leaves feeling overlooked, as if the interaction's lifeblood had been drained, leaving behind a sense of frustration and disconnection. Effective communication doesn't only serve as a bridge; it is also a salve, essential during challenging situations. Consider a tense moment where a guest feels slighted.

A sincere, well-timed apology can quickly de-escalate the situation, restoring trust, much like how oxygen replenishes and heals the body.

However, if the apology is robotic, without warmth or eye contact, it can backfire, amplifying the guest's irritation.

A lack of genuine connection in these moments can damage trust, making the guest feel disregarded instead of valued.

Whether spoken or unspoken, effective communication requires active listening, careful observation of non-verbal cues, and a willingness to respond thoughtfully, ensuring that the interaction aligns with the guest's emotions and needs.

It requires an attentiveness that may seem subtle but is transformative, showing the guest that they are not merely a transaction but someone whose comfort and satisfaction matter deeply.

When communication falters, even small missteps can disrupt the guest experience, underscoring the critical need for precision and presence.

Yet, when communication is executed thoughtfully, it becomes a pillar of trust and satisfaction. It allows hospitality professionals to bring warmth and authenticity to each interaction, reinforcing the human touch that lies at the heart of service excellence.

As effective communication sets the stage for every exchange, it also prepares hospitality professionals for adaptability, ensuring they can pivot gracefully in an industry where no two days, or guests, are ever quite the same.

Chapter Three: **Adaptability**

No Two Days are the same

Adaptability in service excellence is like a seasoned sailor's skill in reading the unpredictable seas.

Just as sailors masterfully respond to shifting tides and changing weather, hospitality professionals rise to the challenges and surprises that each guest interaction brings.

Adaptability isn't just a skill—it's an instinct, an ability to balance preparation with the freedom to adjust and innovate on the spot, ensuring that each guest experience remains as flawless and memorable as possible.

In a world where no two guests are the same, adaptability serves as a guiding light, turning unexpected situations into opportunities to exceed expectations.

Picture a bustling restaurant where a guest arrives without any prior mention of a severe food allergy. This kind of last-minute need could easily throw the kitchen off balance, but for an adaptable chef, it becomes an opportunity to showcase skill and care. Rather than viewing the dietary restriction as an obstacle, the chef sees a chance to personalize the experience.

By personally connecting with the guest to understand their needs, the chef not only ensures safety but crafts a delicious alternative that celebrates the guest's preferences.

This is the art of adaptability in motion: a swift pivot that doesn't just save the experience but transforms it into a moment of unique care and culinary creativity. Such an approach leaves the guest feeling seen, valued, and understood in a way that goes far beyond the meal itself.

In another scenario, imagine a guest from a culture with dining traditions different from the restaurant's typical approach.

They may prefer certain ingredients or specific types of service that are not immediately standard. An adaptable server listens actively and adjusts without hesitation, finding ways to honor these preferences and make the guest feel at home.

Perhaps this involves offering a specific type of tea or altering the pace of the meal to allow for longer conversations. These thoughtful gestures, driven by adaptability, become powerful symbols of cultural respect.
By making small but meaningful adjustments, the hospitality professional doesn't just meet expectations; they show that the guest's comfort is central, no matter where they are from.

Or consider a fine dining event where a dinner menu change occurs at the last moment due to a missing ingredient.

The restaurant staff, guided by adaptability, springs into action, each team member knowing their role in communicating the change, adjusting timing, and informing the guests.

When guests experience this level of composure and creativity in the face of disruption, their impression of the restaurant is not diminished but rather enhanced. The team's adaptability, rather than the problem itself, becomes the takeaway, fostering loyalty and trust.

Adaptability in hospitality is about staying fluid, open, and agile. It is about embracing each moment as a fresh opportunity to connect, satisfy, and inspire.

When a hospitality professional approaches their work with adaptability, they move beyond standardized service to a realm where service becomes an art form—where each adjustment, each quick decision, and each tailored response builds an experience that resonates.

In a fast-paced, ever-changing industry, adaptability is what sustains the heartbeat of true hospitality, keeping service resilient, agile, and authentically guest-centered.

As we transition into the next chapter, we see how a positive attitude is the natural companion to adaptability. Adaptability equips us to respond effectively to change, while a positive attitude brings energy, enthusiasm, and warmth to those responses.

Together, they create an environment where every interaction, no matter how challenging, becomes an opportunity to uplift and inspire.

These qualities, in harmony, are the foundation of service excellence, infusing the guest experience with moments of memorable connection and genuine care.

*Chapter Four: **Positive Attitude***

The Power of Optimism

A positive attitude is the consciousness of service excellence, infusing each interaction, every task, and every experience with warmth, optimism, and genuine care.

It goes beyond just offering a smile or kind words; it's a consistent, wholehearted mind-set that permeates one's work, shaping how guests are treated, how team members support each other, and how challenges are faced.

With a positive outlook, each interaction becomes an opportunity to uplift and inspire, creating an atmosphere where guests feel cherished and team members find motivation and camaraderie.

Picture a guest arriving at a hotel on their birthday, only to discover their room isn't ready due to an unexpected delay. Such moments could easily sour the guest's special day.

However, the front desk staff, radiating positivity and genuine hospitality, warmly greets the guest with an enthusiastic smile, apologizes sincerely, and offers a complimentary upgrade. To celebrate the guest's birthday, they arrange for a thoughtful gift—a bottle of sparkling wine and a handwritten card.

The staff's positive attitude transforms what could have been a disappointing experience into a memorable celebration, elevating an ordinary check-in to a moment of sincere joy and connection.

In this moment, positivity doesn't just save the experience; it enhances it, creating a cherished memory for the guest.

Now, imagine a busy day in the hotel's restaurant, where an unexpected rush of guests strains the team. Amidst the chaos, the restaurant manager embodies a steady, encouraging attitude, stepping in to assist the team.

They manage not only tasks but also morale, fostering calm and purpose among the staff with their positivity. They acknowledge small victories, encourage laughter, and support everyone with praise, making the busy environment feel like a collective effort rather than a high-stress challenge.

This optimistic leadership doesn't just motivate the team; it creates an uplifting experience that guests can sense and appreciate. Even in a crowded dining room, guests feel welcome and cared for, knowing that the team's dedication shines through in every detail.

In the broader context of hospitality, a positive attitude transforms the mundane into the memorable. When hospitality professionals view their role with positivity, they see each interaction as a chance to leave a lasting impact.

This mind-set helps create an environment where everyone feels welcomed and cared for, from guests who walk through the doors to team members working alongside each other. Guests can feel the uplifting energy, often leaving with a sense of connection and delight that goes far beyond the quality of the service itself.

When leaders and team members model positivity, it becomes contagious, fostering a work environment where team members rally together with resilience and joy.

Challenges are no longer obstacles; they're opportunities for teamwork and celebration, no matter how small the victories.

Guests, in turn, recognize this uplifting energy and are more likely to return, knowing they can expect more than just good service—they can anticipate an experience full of warmth, sincerity, and care.

In the end, a positive attitude is more than a professional asset—it's a way of life.

It's a conscious choice to see the best in every situation, to lift those around you, and to approach each day with purpose and enthusiasm. In hospitality, where every interaction shapes someone's experience, positivity is the foundation of service excellence.

It fosters an environment where guests and team members alike feel valued, appreciated, and genuinely connected.

As we transition to the next chapter, we explore the role of patience in service excellence.

While positivity sets the tone for memorable experiences, patience ensures that each interaction is met with care and attentiveness.

Patience allows us to manage expectations gracefully, resolve issues thoughtfully, and provide a level of attentive service that enriches every guest interaction.

good vibes

Chapter Five: **Patience**

The Art of Composure

Patience in hospitality is akin to the careful strategy of a chess game, where each move requires thoughtful consideration and calm focus.

Just as a skilled chess player looks beyond the immediate move, envisioning the entire board and planning for success, a hospitality professional must see the bigger picture, anticipating guest needs, handling unexpected challenges, and fostering an atmosphere of calm and care.

This patience, a true art in service, becomes the foundation of every positive guest interaction, transforming potential frustrations into opportunities for genuine connection.

Imagine a bustling hotel kitchen during the dinner rush, where orders stack up and wait times lengthen. A patient team member handles the pressure with grace, communicating with guests about the delay and offering a complimentary drink or appetizer to ease their experience.

Much like a chess player considering every possible move, this hospitality professional looks at the options available to make the guest's experience as seamless as possible, valuing the long game of guest satisfaction over immediate convenience.

Their patience turns a stressful situation into a moment of trust-building, showing the guest that they are valued, not forgotten.

Consider, too, the case of a guest who is indecisive about their meal, spending considerable time choosing and asking questions about the menu.

The server, displaying genuine patience, listens attentively, answers every question, and offers gentle suggestions to guide the guest's choice.

This calm, attentive approach reassures the guest, making them feel heard rather than hurried. The patience shown here creates a positive connection, building rapport that could make this guest a regular visitor who appreciates the thoughtful care they receive.

In hospitality, patience is often about playing the long game...

Just as a chess player understands that victory comes through a series of calculated moves, hospitality professionals know that lasting guest loyalty and satisfaction are cultivated over time.

When each guest interaction is met with patience and care, guests feel respected, appreciated, and likely to return, reinforcing the establishment's reputation for exceptional service.

Every patient response adds up, creating a long-term relationship built on trust and understanding, much like the gradual progression toward checkmate.

Yet patience isn't just about the guest; it also strengthens the team dynamic.

In a busy restaurant or hotel, impatient reactions can spread stress and tension, affecting not only the team's mood but also the guest experience.

Rushed decisions or poorly handled complaints can have lasting negative effects, turning minor issues into major disappointments.

When patience is prioritized, however, hospitality professionals become more thoughtful in their actions, creating a harmonious, positive environment where both guests and team members feel supported.

Handling each scenario with patience ensures that every action is deliberate and impactful, contributing to a smoother, more enjoyable experience for everyone.

By embracing patience, hospitality professionals turn what could be frustrations into memorable moments, navigating challenges with the finesse of a skilled chess player planning each move with confidence.

In the next chapter, we'll delve into problem-solving—the natural partner of patience.

While patience sets the stage for calm, focused interactions, effective problem-solving transforms obstacles into opportunities, elevating service excellence and turning challenges into moments of triumph.

Chapter Six: **Problem-Solving**

Navigating Challenges

Problem-solving in hospitality transcends mere skill; it serves as the essential toolkit for delivering service excellence.

Each day presents a myriad of unforeseen challenges—ranging from minor inconveniences to major disruptions—and the ability to navigate these effectively is what sets exceptional service apart from the ordinary.

Hospitality professionals must tackle every challenge with the precision and calm of a seasoned paramedic, ready to spring into action at a moment's notice.

Take, for instance, the scenario of a guest who suddenly realizes they've left their important travel documents in their hotel room just hours before their flight.

The concierge team springs into action, coordinating with housekeeping to locate the documents, while also arranging for express delivery to the airport.

This prompt and efficient response not only alleviates a potentially stressful situation but also exemplifies outstanding problem-solving skills, ensuring the guest's travel plans proceed smoothly.

It's the human touch—the genuine concern and swift action—that transforms a moment of panic into one of relief, reinforcing the guest's sense of trust in the establishment.

Now, imagine the bustling atmosphere of a hotel restaurant on a busy public holiday. The kitchen and front-of-house staff are working in perfect harmony, serving guests with a seamless flow of service.

Suddenly, a large group arrives to celebrate a 70th birthday, only to find that their reservation has mysteriously vanished from the system.

In this moment of crisis, staying calm is crucial. The staff must quickly mobilize, informing both the kitchen and the bar about the unexpected influx while ensuring they are prepared for increased demand.

The front-of-house team works efficiently to reconfigure the dining area, rearranging tables and reallocating bookings to accommodate the large party.

Throughout this process, clear and empathetic communication is essential.

A sincere apology for the mix-up, accompanied by immediate solutions—such as complimentary welcome drinks or antipasti—demonstrates that the guests' comfort and experience are the top priorities.

The consequences of mishandling this scenario can be dire.

If the situation is not addressed effectively, the group may encounter long waits, poor service, or even be left without a table.

Such missteps not only ruin their special celebration but can also tarnish the restaurant's reputation. Seated guests may perceive the establishment as disorganized, which can deter future business.

Yet, in this high-pressure scenario, effective problem-solving transforms a potential disaster into an opportunity to shine. Each challenge—big or small—becomes a chance to reaffirm a commitment to guest satisfaction.

Successful problem-solving not only resolves the immediate issue but also cultivates a sense of reliability and confidence among guests.

When patrons witness or experience this level of responsive care, they feel valued and reassured, knowing that the establishment is well-equipped to handle any situation with competence and compassion.

This trust fosters lasting connections, encouraging guests to return, confident that their needs will be met—even when things don't go as planned.

Complementing problem-solving is a keen attention to detail, which ensures that every element of service contributes to a seamless and memorable experience.

The little things matter: from remembering a guest's name to noting their preferences, these details enhance the overall service and show that the staff is genuinely invested in each guest's experience.

Together, problem-solving and attention to detail form the backbone of service excellence, where no challenge is too great, and no detail too small to matter.

They create an environment where hospitality professionals are empowered to respond with creativity and empathy, turning obstacles into opportunities for connection and loyalty.

In the next chapter, we will delve into the significance of attention to detail in hospitality. Just as a well-orchestrated symphony relies on each musician playing in harmony, attention to detail would be the conductor keeping the beat.

Chapter Seven: **Attention to Detail**

Perfecting the Experience

Attention to detail is the symphony of service excellence, where each element must play in perfect harmony to create an unforgettable experience.

This metaphorical symphony is not merely a collection of isolated notes; it is about how each note interacts with others to form a cohesive and beautiful melody that resonates with every guest.

Imagine the ambiance of an elegant gala.

The table is not just arranged; it is curated with the precision of a composer crafting a masterpiece.

Each element—silverware, glassware, floral arrangements, and seating—is placed with exactness that reflects a deep understanding of how these details combine to elevate the overall experience.

The ambiance must be a feast for the senses, where sight, sound, and taste intertwine seamlessly.

Attention to detail is achieved not when there is nothing more to add, but when nothing is absent; what remains is flawless. It is a skill that demands both consistency and precision.

Consistency ensures that the quality of service never wavers, creating an environment where guests feel a sense of familiarity and comfort.

Precision, on the other hand, involves executing each detail with such meticulousness that it becomes almost imperceptible to the observer; yet, its absence would be immediately felt, like a missing note in a symphony.

In the hospitality industry, when attention to detail is flawless, every element harmonizes seamlessly, creating a magical experience that feels both organized and heartfelt.

It is in these moments that the human touch becomes apparent—where the staff goes beyond the expected, noticing the nuances that enhance the guest experience.

This seamless harmony is what guests come to expect; it is the standard against which they measure their experience. Any deviation from this standard—no matter how minor—can lead to dissatisfaction.

Consider, for instance, a high-profile wine and food pairing event featuring a renowned winemaker and a celebrated chef collaborating on an exclusive evening.

The setting is nothing short of spectacular, complete with elegant table settings, expertly crafted menus, and a carefully curated selection of wines.

Yet, as the main course is served, a subtle but significant issue arises—the second red wine glass, intended for the paired wine of the main course, is missing.

This seemingly small oversight disrupts the flow of the evening, much like a missing instrument would throw an orchestra into disarray.

While the rest of the meal may proceed without incident, this absent note affects the overall harmony of the event, casting a shadow over the evening's successes.

Guests may recall the exquisite flavors of the meal, yet their memories might be tainted by the small lapse in detail, highlighting how crucial every element is to the overall experience.

In hospitality, the difference between a meal and a dining experience, between a stay and a memorable getaway, lies in the degree of attention to detail.

When executed flawlessly, attention to detail does more than impress; it creates emotional connections between guests and the service staff, fostering loyalty and trust.

As attention to detail harmonizes the guest experience, resilience sustains service excellence amidst adversity.

It is the quiet force that keeps service in order, ensuring that the symphony of hospitality continues uninterrupted, even when challenges arise.

This resilience is reflected in the ability to adapt, to reconfigure and reallocate resources to ensure that no detail is overlooked, even in the face of unexpected hurdles.

Ultimately, attention to detail is the visual manifestation of love for hospitality.

It transforms the ordinary into the extraordinary, turning a simple meal into a cherished memory and a routine stay into a retreat that lingers in the hearts of guests long after they have left.

By recognizing the importance of the human touch in every detail, hospitality professionals can create experiences that not only meet but exceed expectations, leaving an indelible mark on those they serve.

In the next chapter, we will explore the essence of resilience in hospitality—the spirit of endurance that binds every interaction, ensuring that the symphony of service excellence remains in perfect tune.

Chapter Eight - ***Resilience***

The Quiet Strength

Resilience is the gravitational force of service excellence—often invisible, yet profoundly impactful.

It emerges in moments of adversity, providing hospitality professionals with the strength to rebound from challenges and maintain high service standards, even under less-than-ideal conditions.

Imagine a bustling restaurant on a Friday night, where the energy is palpable, and the dining room buzzes with chatter.

A server is managing a full section of tables when chaos ensues: the kitchen misplaces an order, they're down a staff member, and it's the third consecutive double shift.

Amid this whirlwind, one table becomes particularly animated as a guest expresses frustration over an incorrect order.

Despite the mounting pressure, the server embodies calm and composure. They listen attentively to the guest's concerns, radiating genuine empathy. In this moment, the server becomes a pillar of strength, reassuring the guest and quickly relaying the issue to the kitchen.

Their ability to stay focused and resilient in the face of challenges transforms a potential negative experience into a positive one.

When the guest leaves satisfied, appreciating the personal attention and care, it is a testament to the server's quiet strength and steadfast resilience. Just as gravity exerts a constant force to keep planets in their orbits, individual resilience provides the steady influence needed to navigate professional challenges without allowing them to disrupt the broader team dynamic.

When one person remains composed, it fosters an environment where everyone can work together more effectively, regardless of external pressures.

At the team level, resilience becomes even more critical. Picture a high-profile wedding reception in full swing when a sudden power outage plunges the venue into darkness.

The atmosphere, once vibrant with laughter and music, now hangs in uncertainty.

Yet, instead of succumbing to panic, the kitchen staff maintains their composure, quickly assessing menu options that can be prepared without power. They communicate these changes to the front-of-house team, who are equally unfazed.

As the wait staff relay the adapted menu to the guests, they do so with calm assurance, lighting candles to create a romantic and intimate atmosphere.

This unexpected turn of events, initially a potential disaster, transforms into a unique and enchanting experience. The couple and their guests leave not only celebrating the wedding but cherishing the resilience and grace exhibited by the team during the unexpected challenge.

Resilience is deeply rooted in both individual and collective capacity.

Individual resilience empowers staff to manage personal challenges without letting them impact the team dynamic, while collective resilience unifies the team, keeping everyone focused on the common goal.

The absence of resilience can lead to significant setbacks; much like a lack of gravity would cause celestial bodies to drift apart, the absence of resilience can result in a fragmented team.

Consider how minor issues, like a reservation running late or a VIP guest arriving unexpectedly, can escalate into major problems without a cohesive response.

If staff members lack resilience, the team may struggle to adapt, leading to confusion and frustration. In contrast, a resilient team not only survives challenges but thrives, ensuring that high-quality service is consistently delivered.

Ultimately, the ability to bounce back from setbacks and continue performing at a high level distinguishes exceptional teams from the rest.

Resilience, paired with the human touch, fosters an environment where staff members feel empowered to support one another, creating a safety net that elevates service standards and enhances the overall

guest experience.

As we transition to the next chapter, we will delve deeper into how teamwork builds on the foundation of resilience, illustrating how a cohesive team can navigate challenges and deliver exceptional service through collaboration and shared strength.

Chapter Nine – **Teamwork**

The Muscle Power

Teamwork is the muscle power behind service excellence, providing the strength, endurance, and coordination necessary to transform individual efforts into a cohesive, extraordinary guest experience.

Just as muscles work together to enable movement, a well-coordinated team drives the smooth operation of a hospitality establishment, ensuring that each guest feels valued and well cared for.

Consider a bustling hotel during a major event. Guests are arriving in waves, the restaurant is fully booked, and the housekeeping team is working tirelessly to prepare rooms.

Suddenly, a key team member is involved in a serious car accident and cannot make it to work. In this critical moment, the team faces the immediate challenge of covering additional responsibilities while maintaining the high standards of service that guests expect.

Here, teamwork becomes the sinew that keeps the operation running smoothly. Each department must quickly reassess its resources and workload for the day, reallocating available assistance to the affected department.

This swift adaptation and mutual support exemplify the strength of teamwork in action, showcasing how collaboration can turn potential setbacks into opportunities for growth and unity.

Effective teamwork goes beyond merely filling immediate gaps; it involves handling challenges with a collaborative mind-set.

While individual resilience is crucial in overcoming obstacles, it is teamwork that amplifies this strength. When a team member is absent, the collective effort ensures that service remains consistent, demonstrating how teamwork helps maintain high standards even in the face of significant disruptions.

Transitioning smoothly between the roles of a team player and a leader is vital in these scenarios.

Team members might step up to take on additional responsibilities or offer guidance and support to their colleagues.
This flexibility allows operations to continue seamlessly, even during unforeseen challenges.

The human touch in service excellence shines through in these moments, as empathy and camaraderie elevate the entire team's performance.

Creating a culture of mutual respect and collaboration is essential for successful teamwork. In a diverse team, understanding and appreciating each other's strengths fosters a positive work environment.

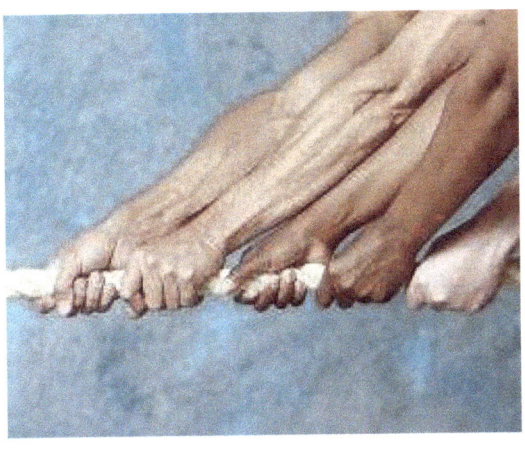

Leaders who recognize and leverage each team member's unique talents will cultivate a team that not only functions efficiently but thrives in every situation.

Celebrating moments of success—such as positive guest feedback or the successful management of a high-pressure event—strengthens team bonds and motivates everyone to continue delivering exceptional service.

Teamwork is not merely about dividing tasks; it is about coming together to amplify collective strength.

When a team stands united, they not only share the load but ignite the spark of creativity and unparalleled service.

It is this unity and collaborative spirit that elevates their efforts from ordinary to extraordinary, ensuring that every guest experience is truly exceptional.

Just as muscles grow stronger with regular exercise, a commitment to continuous learning drives the evolution of service excellence.

In an industry characterized by constant change, ongoing education and skill development are essential for staying ahead of trends and maintaining high standards.

When team members engage in continuous learning, they share knowledge and skills that further enhance their collaboration, creating a cycle of improvement that benefits everyone.

As we transition to the next chapter, we will explore how continuous learning fuels the ongoing evolution of service excellence, showcasing the ways in which teams can grow and adapt to meet the ever-changing demands of the hospitality industry.

Together, with a commitment to teamwork and a focus on the human touch, we can ensure that service excellence remains a cornerstone of our industry.

Chapter Ten: **Continuous Learning**

Evolving Excellence

Continuous learning is essential for growth and adaptation in the dynamic world of hospitality, akin to how evolution ensures survival and success in an ever-changing environment.

This journey of knowledge involves staying informed about industry developments, seeking feedback, and striving for both personal and professional improvement.

The relentless pursuit of knowledge helps professionals and organizations remain at the forefront of their field, enabling them to respond effectively to the evolving needs and expectations of their guests.

Consider a luxury hotel that consistently ranks high in guest satisfaction. This achievement stems from a robust culture of continuous learning.

Staff members are encouraged to enhance their skills and stay updated with the latest industry trends by attending workshops on new technologies, participating in customer service seminars, and engaging in leadership training.

This commitment not only helps maintain high standards but also fosters innovation, enabling the hotel to exceed guest expectations and create memorable experiences.

Continuous learning applies to every aspect of hospitality service.

Imagine a server who has recently completed a course in first aid. During a busy dinner service, the atmosphere shifts dramatically when a guest suddenly begins to choke on their food.

The server, drawing on their recent training, remains composed and performs the Heimlich maneuver with precision, helping the guest dislodge the obstruction.

As the guest begins to breathe again, the server maintains a calm and reassuring presence, offers a glass of water, and checks in to ensure their well-being, all while alerting the restaurant manager for further assistance.

This quick and confident application of first aid skills not only resolves a potentially dangerous situation but also underscores the critical role of continuous learning in ensuring guest safety and maintaining high service standards under pressure.

Similarly, consider a chef who continuously experiments with new recipes and stays abreast of culinary trends, ensuring that the menu remains fresh and appealing.

Servers who partake in training programs to deepen their understanding of wine pairings, menu items, and service techniques can enhance the dining experience with refined knowledge and personalized recommendations.
The human touch in these interactions—rooted in empathy and understanding—transforms a simple meal into a delightful experience that guests will cherish.

Another vital aspect of continuous learning lies in the constructive criticism and feedback received from guests. Each interaction offers a wealth of insights that can illuminate areas for improvement and spark innovation.

For example, if a guest expresses dissatisfaction with a particular dish or service element, the team can view this feedback as a valuable opportunity for growth rather than a setback.

By actively listening and responding to such feedback, staff can refine their approaches, tailor their services to meet guest preferences, and ultimately enhance the overall experience.

This commitment to learning from guests not only fosters a culture of accountability but also empowers staff to develop their skills further, ensuring that each encounter contributes to a cycle of continuous improvement.

Adopting a mind-set of curiosity and openness is essential for practicing continuous learning.

This mind-set involves actively seeking new knowledge, adapting to changes, and viewing every experience as an opportunity for growth.

When hospitality professionals embody this approach, they embark on an ongoing journey of improvement and adaptation, highlighting that excellence is not a fixed destination but a continual process of refinement.

Conversely, a lack of commitment to growth can lead to stagnation, outdated practices, and decreased service quality.

In a field where standards are constantly evolving, failing to embrace continuous learning can result in falling behind competitors and missing out on opportunities for improvement.

The ability to learn and adapt is a defining characteristic of successful hospitality establishments.

By fostering a culture of curiosity and ongoing education, hospitality professionals contribute to exceptional guest experiences, ensuring that the industry remains vibrant and competitive.

The human touch—marked by genuine care, empathy, and a commitment to improvement—enhances every interaction and solidifies the bond between service providers and guests.

As we conclude this chapter, remember that the journey of continuous learning is not just about acquiring knowledge; it's about enriching the human experience.

It's a commitment to service excellence that empowers every individual in the hospitality industry to innovate, grow, and inspire others, ensuring that each guest encounter is not only memorable but truly exceptional.

Conclusion

In an era where artificial intelligence increasingly shapes our daily interactions, the essence of exceptional service in the hospitality industry remains profoundly human.

As we navigate a world where AI can process information with unmatched speed and accuracy, it becomes crucial to reaffirm the importance of the ten human qualities that define true service excellence.

Empathy, effective communication, adaptability, a positive attitude, patience, problem-solving skills, attention to detail, resilience, teamwork, and a commitment to continuous learning are not mere traits; they are the essence of service excellence that transcends algorithms and automation.

These qualities embody the depth of human connection and understanding—an intricate tapestry of emotions and experiences that AI, despite its advancements, cannot replicate.

Empathy stands as the cornerstone of service excellence, allowing us to genuinely connect with guests and understand their needs on a personal level. In a world often characterized by digital exchanges, the ability to listen deeply and respond with heartfelt concern creates an unparalleled bond between service providers and guests.

Effective communication further builds these bridges, fostering clarity and trust through authentic interactions. It's the simple act of asking about a guest's day or sharing a personal recommendation that transforms a transactional encounter into a memorable experience.

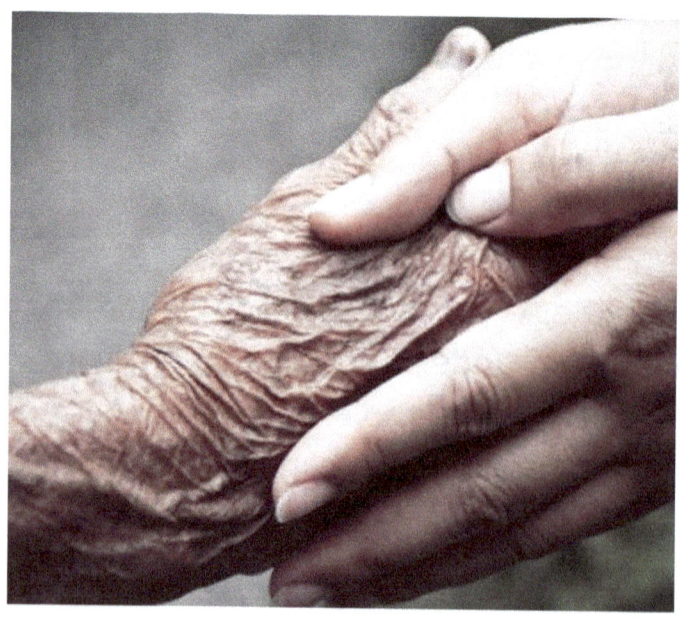

Adaptability ensures that we can respond to changing circumstances with grace and flexibility, whether it's adjusting to a guest's unique requests or navigating unexpected challenges.

A positive attitude infuses every interaction with optimism and warmth, making guests feel valued and welcome, while patience guarantees that each individual feels heard and understood.

These human qualities create a nurturing environment where guests can relax and enjoy their experiences.

Moreover, problem-solving skills empower us to navigate challenges and exceed expectations.

The ability to think creatively and implement solutions on the fly is something that defines truly exceptional service.

Attention to detail further enhances the guest experience, ensuring that every aspect—down to the placement of a napkin or the selection of a welcome drink—is meticulously crafted with care.

Resilience provides the strength to overcome obstacles and maintain high standards, allowing teams to bounce back from setbacks and deliver consistent excellence.

Teamwork harnesses collective strengths, creating a seamless service experience where each member plays a vital role in the larger mission.

When staff collaborate harmoniously, they amplify the human touch that makes each interaction special.
Lastly, a commitment to continuous learning not only keeps us abreast of industry trends but also encourages personal growth and development, ensuring that we remain adaptable and relevant in a rapidly evolving landscape.

As AI continues to evolve, it's important to remember that while technology can enhance efficiency, it cannot replace the human touch that defines exceptional service.

The hospitality industry has a profound responsibility to perfect, enhance, and celebrate these human qualities. Our mission is to ensure that amidst technological advancements, the human aspects of service are not only preserved but elevated.

By mastering these ten essential qualities, we reaffirm our commitment to the principles of service excellence—where empathy, understanding, and genuine care define our approach to every guest interaction.

The richness of human connection is our greatest asset, allowing us to create experiences that resonate deeply and leave lasting impressions.

As we look to the future, let us embrace the advancements of AI with the understanding that our greatest strength lies in our ability to connect, care, and serve with authenticity and warmth.

In a landscape increasingly dominated by technology, the human touch will always stand as the irreplaceable hallmark of exceptional service.

www.ingramcontent.com/pod-product-compliance
Lightning Source LLC
Chambersburg PA
CBHW070120230526
45472CB00004B/1350